michael bublé

ISBN: 978-1-5400-4346-7

HAL•LEONARD®

Visit Hal Leonard Online at
www.halleonard.com

Contact us:
Hal Leonard
7777 West Bluemound Road
Milwaukee, WI 53213
Email: info@halleonard.com

In Europe, contact:
Hal Leonard Europe Limited
42 Wigmore Street
Marylebone, London, W1U 2RN
Email: info@halleonardeurope.com

In Australia, contact:
Hal Leonard Australia Pty. Ltd.
4 Lentara Court
Cheltenham, Victoria, 3192 Australia
Email: info@halleonard.com.au

WHEN I FALL IN LOVE

Words by EDWARD HEYMAN
Music by VICTOR YOUNG

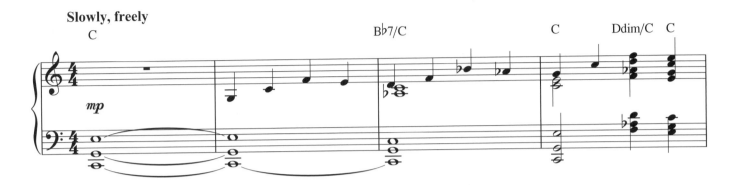

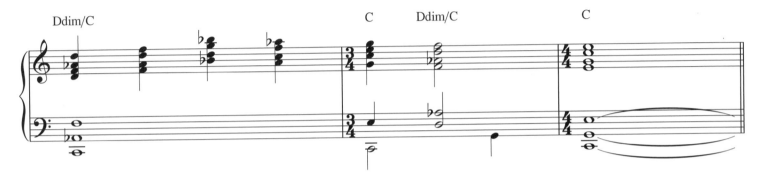

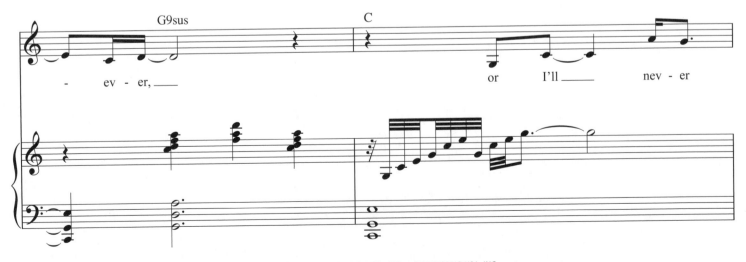

When I give my heart, _____ it will be

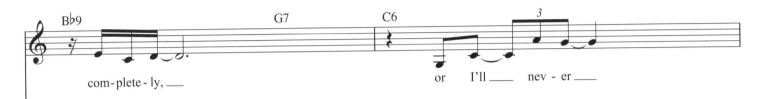

com-plete-ly, _____ or I'll _____ nev-er _____

give _____ my _____ heart. _____

And the mo - ment _____ I _____ can feel that _____

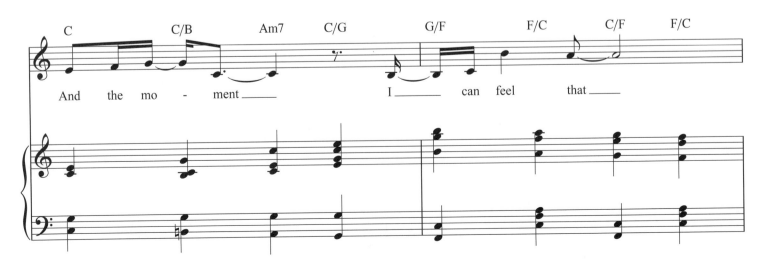

you feel that way too _____ is when I fall in

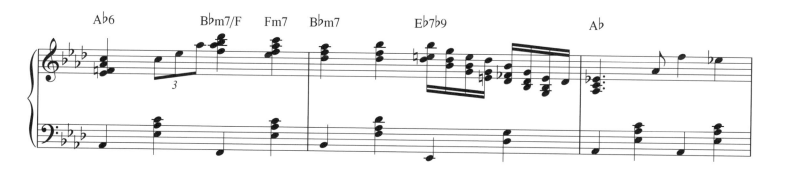

love with you. _____

And _____

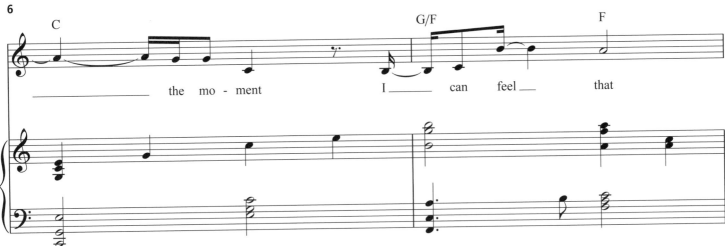

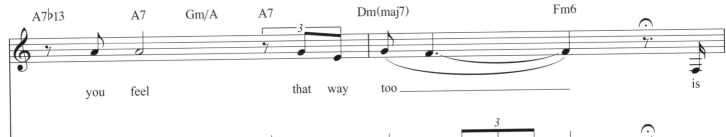

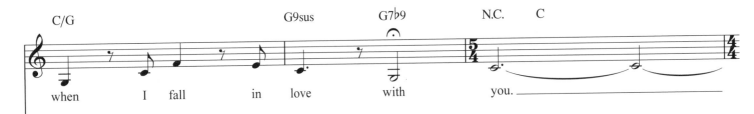

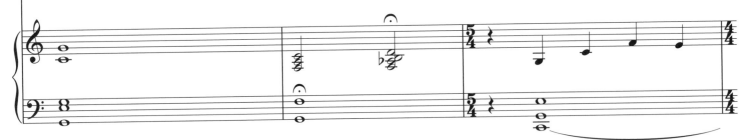

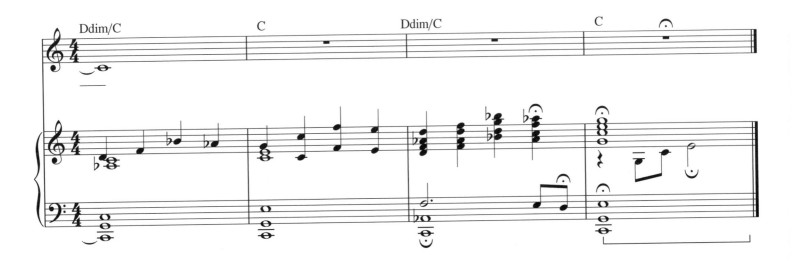

LOVE YOU ANYMORE

Words and Music by SCOTT HARRIS,
ILSEY JUBER, JENS CARLSSON
and CHARLIE PUTH

Just be - cause_ I wan - der 'round_ the plac-

- es we _ would go, _____ hop - ing that _ I'd run _ in - to _ you one _ last

time; just be - cause_ I nev - er took_ your pic -

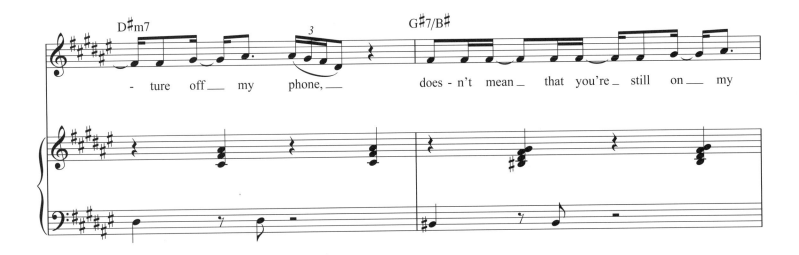

- ture off_ my phone, _ does - n't mean_ that you're_ still on _ my

mind. Just be - cause_ I ac - ci - dent - 'ly slip_

_ and say_ your name _ when I hear_ a song_ that makes_ me in - se - cure; _

just be-cause_ I know_ I'll nev - er ev -

- er feel_ the same,___ does-n't mean I love you an - y -

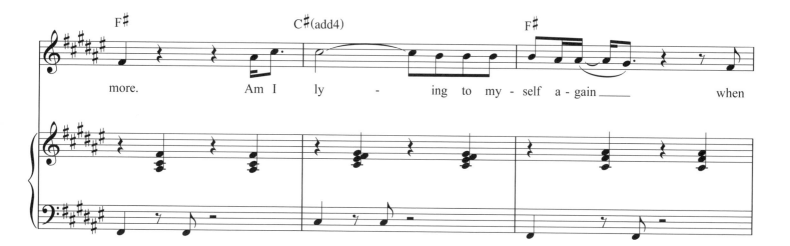

more. Am I ly - ing to my-self a-gain____ when

I say you're not the best I've ev - er had?_____ Am I

ly - ing to my-self a-gain ___ when I say ___ that I'm not miss-ing you so

bad? ___ Just be-cause ___ I'm on ___ my knees ___ and swear -

- ing I ___ will change ___ and I'd do an - y - thing ___ to hear ___ you say, ___ "I'm yours," ___

just be-cause ___ I know ___ I'll nev - er ev -

- er feel the same, doesn't mean I love you an - y - more.

Am I ly - ing to my - self a - gain _____ when I

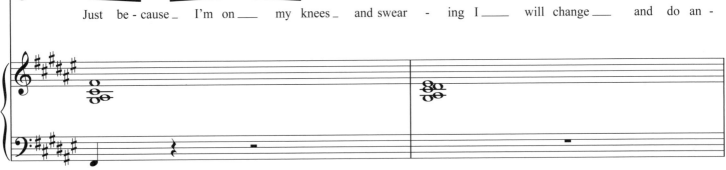

I ONLY HAVE EYES FOR YOU

Words by AL DUBIN
Music by HARRY WARREN

Are the stars ____ out to-night? ____

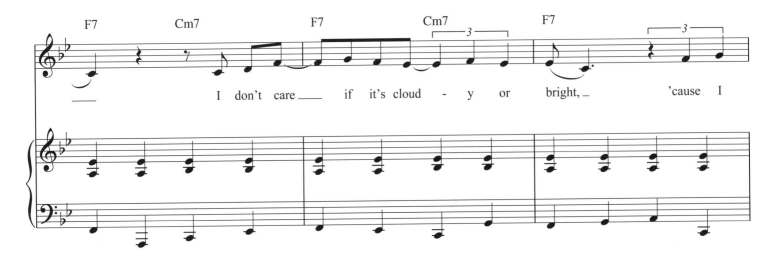

____ I don't care ____ if it's cloud - y or bright, ____ 'cause I

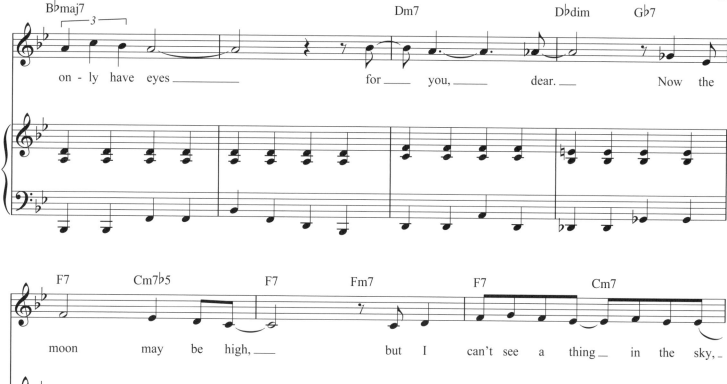

on - ly have eyes _____ for _____ you, _____ dear. _____ Now the

moon may be high, _____ but I can't see a thing _____ in the sky, _____

'cause I on - ly have eyes _____ for _____

you. _____ I don't know

if we're in a _____ gar - den _____

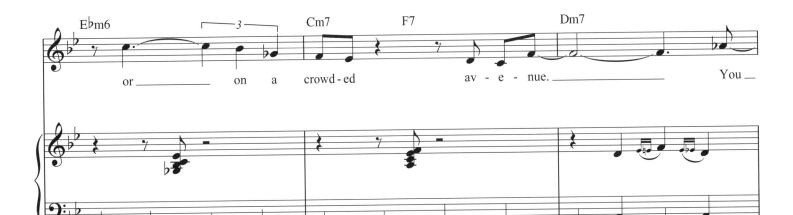

or _____ on a crowd - ed av - e - nue. _____ You _____

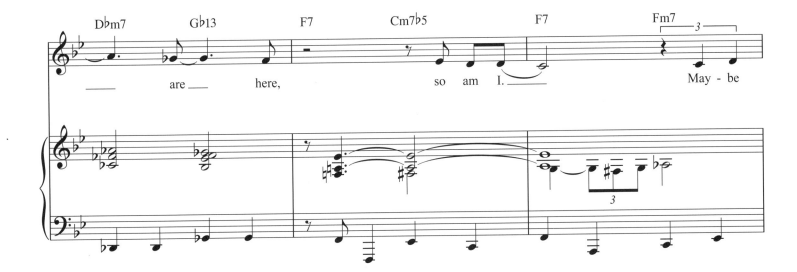

_____ are _____ here, so am I. _____ May - be

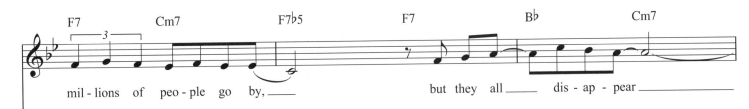

mil - lions of peo - ple go by, _____ but they all _____ dis - ap - pear _____

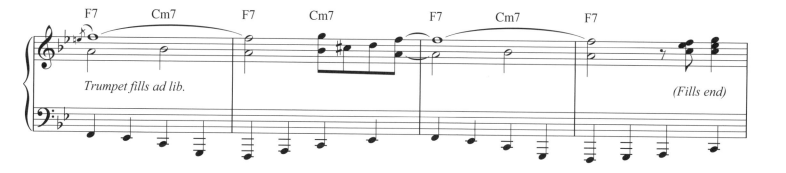

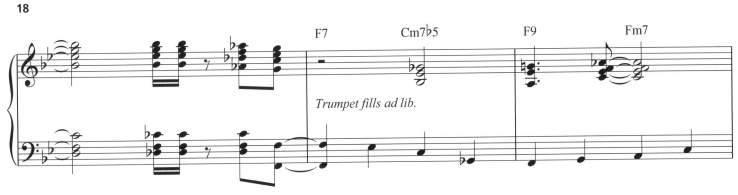

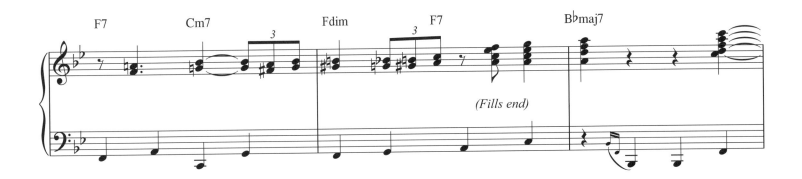

How __ can I live a day __ with - out you? _____

I need your love to see me through.

You're not here by my

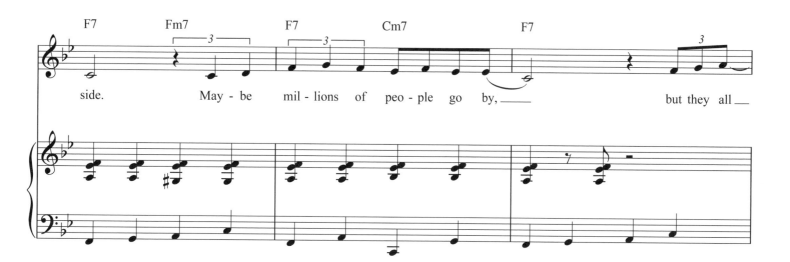

side. May-be mil-lions of peo-ple go by, but they all

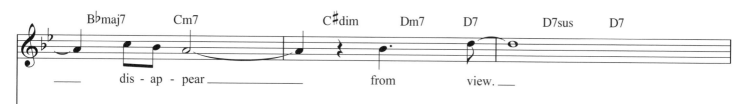

dis-ap-pear from view.

And _____ I on - ly have eyes, _____ I

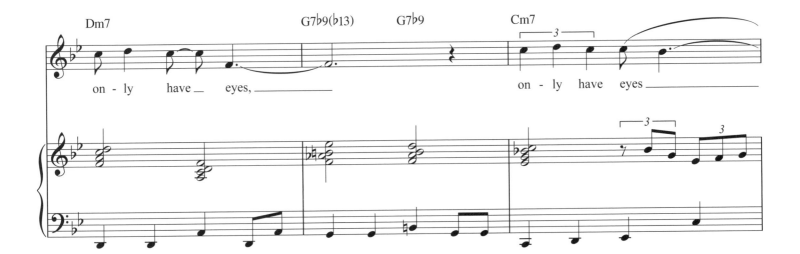

on - ly have _ eyes, _____ on - ly have eyes _____

for ___ you.

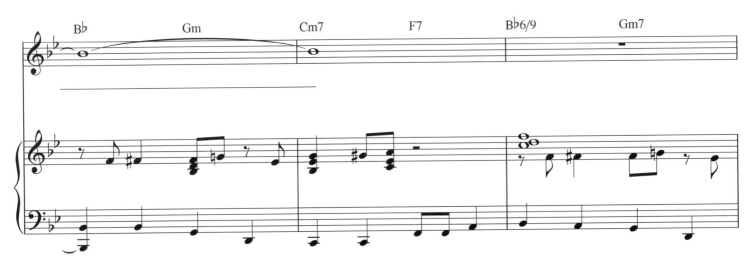

LA VIE EN ROSE
(Take Me to Your Heart Again)

Original French Lyrics by EDITH PIAF
Music by LOUIGUY
English Lyrics by MACK DAVID

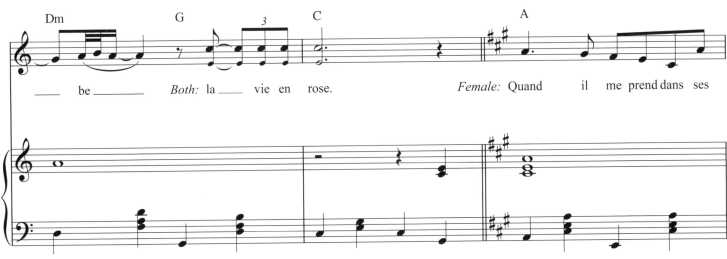

be ___ *Both:* la ___ vie en rose. *Female:* Quand il me prend dans ses

bras, il me par - le de tout bas, je vois la vie en

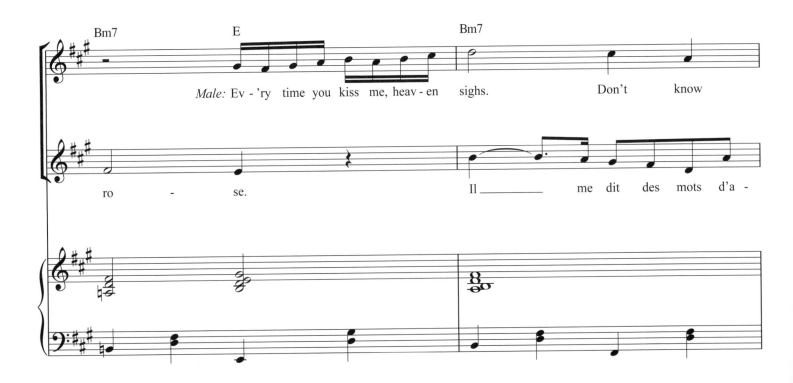

ro - se. *Male:* Ev - 'ry time you kiss me, heav - en sighs. Don't know

Il ___ me dit des mots d'a -

Both: Il est en - tré dans mon cœur, u - ne part de bon - heur, don je con - nais la

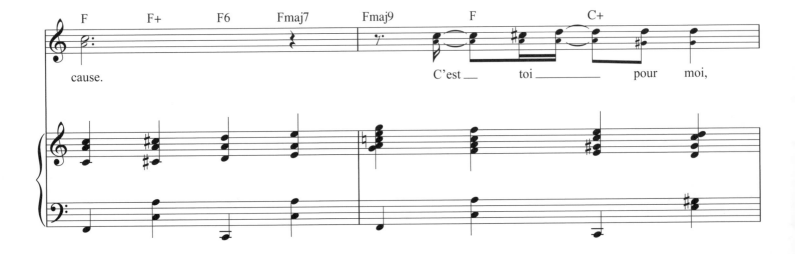

cause. C'est __ toi _____ pour moi,

moi pour toi _____ dans la vie. _____ Il me l'a dit, l'a ju -

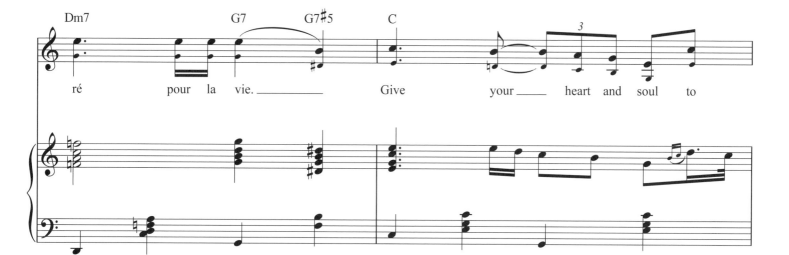

ré pour la vie. _____ Give your _____ heart and soul to

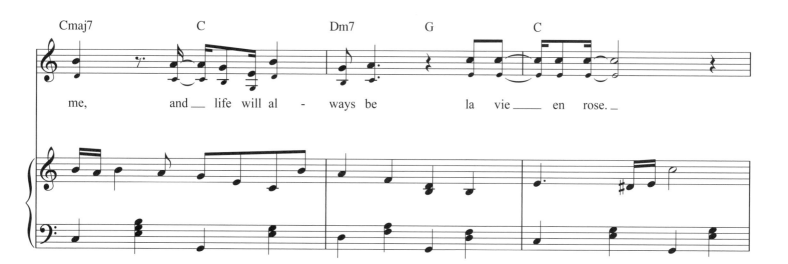

me, and _____ life will al - ways be la vie _____ en rose. _

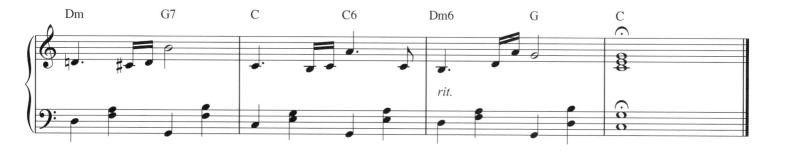

MY FUNNY VALENTINE

Words by LORENZ HART
Music by RICHARD RODGERS

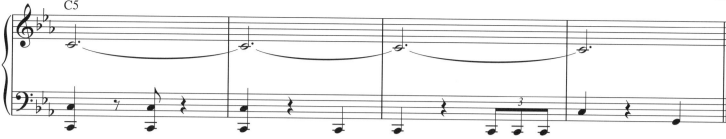

My fun - ny val - en - tine, _____

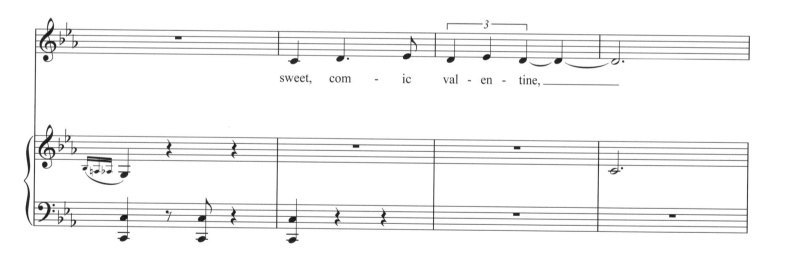

sweet, com - ic val - en - tine, _____

you make _ me smile _____ with my _

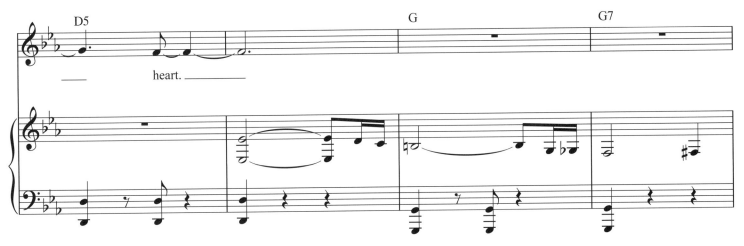

heart.

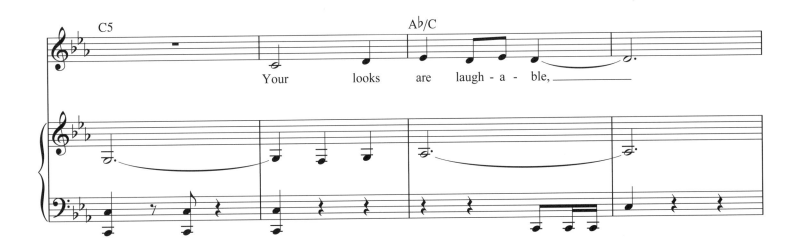

Your looks are laugh-a-ble, _____

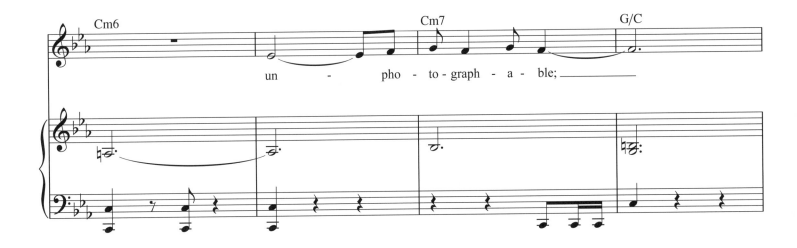

un - pho-to-graph-a-ble; _____

yet you're my _____ fav - 'rite work _ of

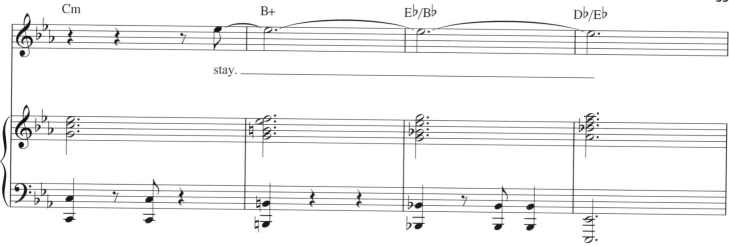

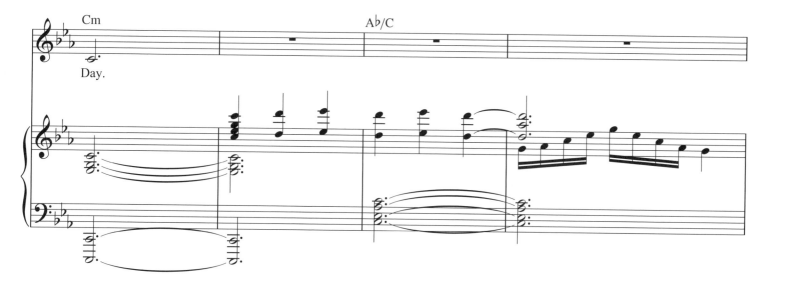

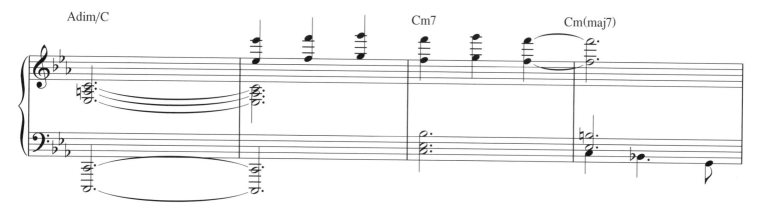

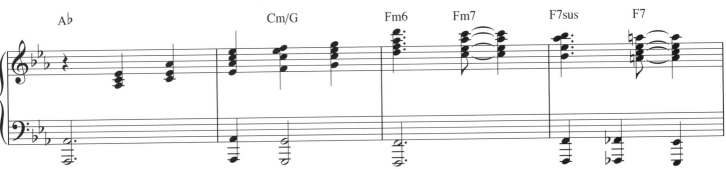

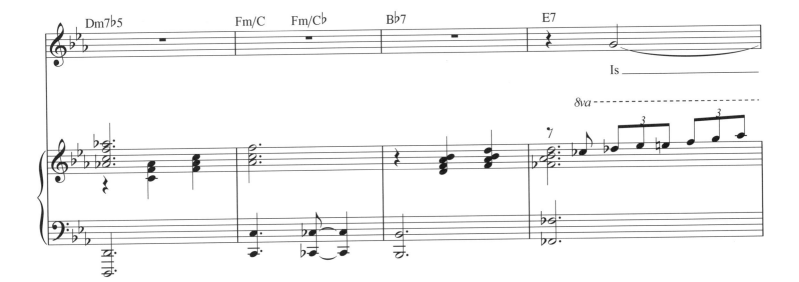

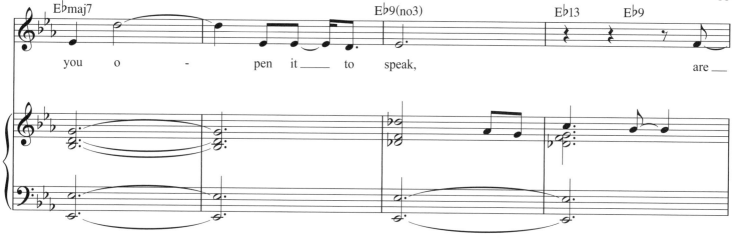

Tempo I (♪♪ = ♪♪)

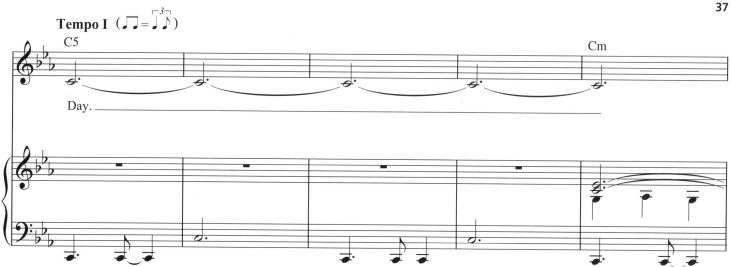

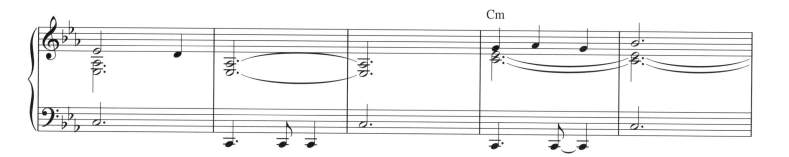

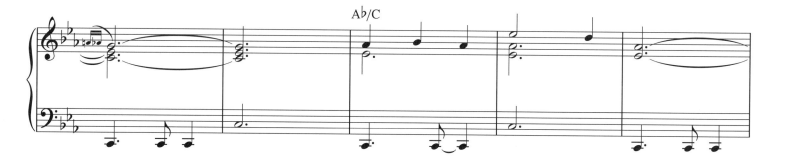

SUCH A NIGHT

Words and Music by
LINCOLN CHASE

It was a night. Oh, __

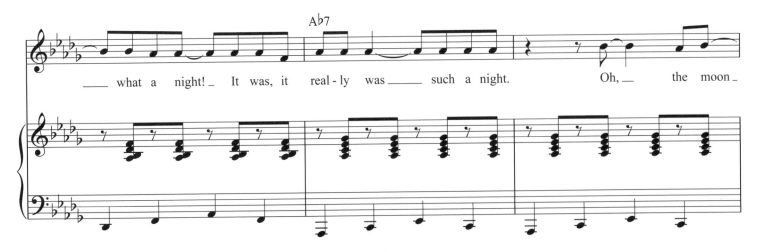

__ what a night! It was, it real-ly was __ such a night. Oh, __ the moon

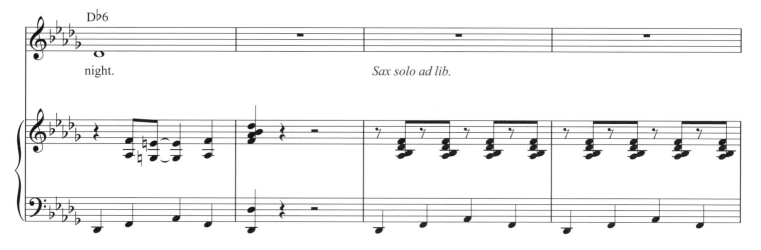

night.   *Sax solo ad lib.*

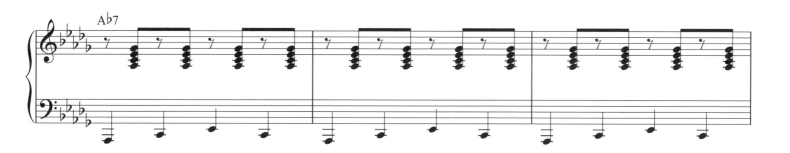

FOREVER NOW

Words and Music by MICHAEL BUBLÉ,
ALAN CHANG, TOM JACKSON
and RYAN LERMAN

No, I'm nev-er gon-na let you down. ___

No mat-ter what you do, ___ I'm for-ev-er proud ___ of you.

I love you for-ev ___ er now. ___

I love you for-ev ___ er now.

HELP ME MAKE IT THROUGH THE NIGHT

Words and Music by
KRIS KRISTOFFERSON

sight). *Both:* And it's sad _____ to be a - lone. _____

Help _____ me make it through _____ the night.

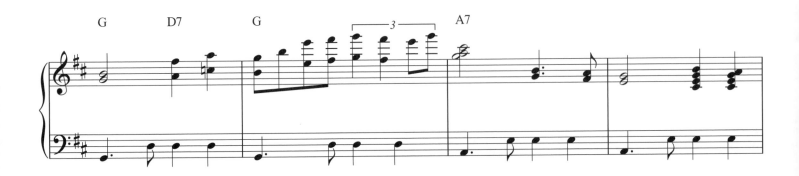

60

UNFORGETTABLE

Words and Music by
IRVING GORDON

Moderately slow, in 4

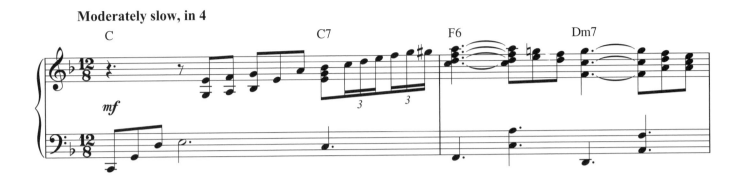

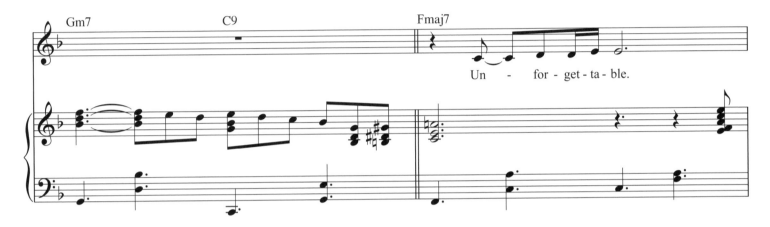

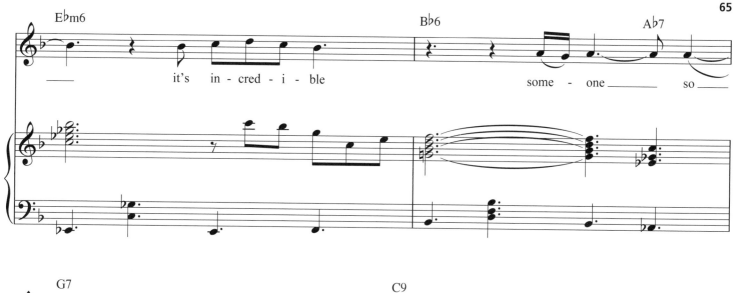

it's in - cred - i - ble   some - one ___ so ___

un - for - get - ta - ble   thinks that I ___ am

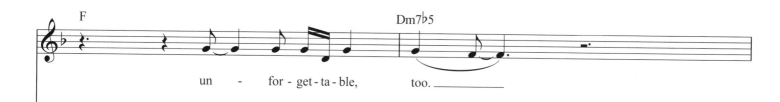

un - for - get - ta - ble,   too. ___

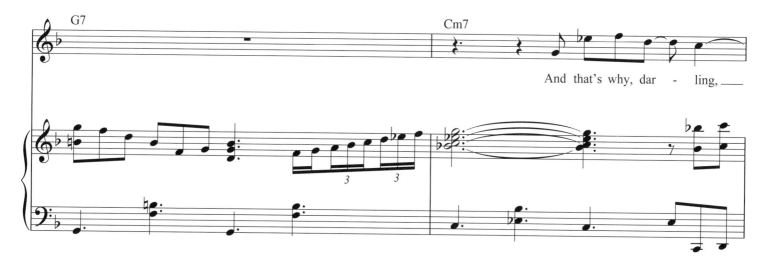

And that's why, dar - ling, ___

when you hold my hand, _____ I _____ can hard -
ly _____ un - der - stand __ how __ some-one like you thinks that I am
un - for - get - ta - ble, too. __

Freely

WHEN YOU'RE SMILING
(The Whole World Smiles with You)

Words and Music by MARK FISHER,
JOE GOODWIN and LARRY SHAY

laugh-ing, babe, _____ when you're laugh-ing,

well, the sun comes shin - ing through. _

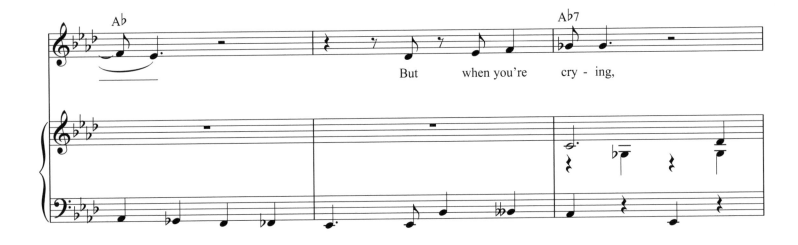

But when you're cry - ing,

you know you _____ bring on _____ the rain. _____ Stop that _

sigh - ing; be _____ hap - py a - gain. ___

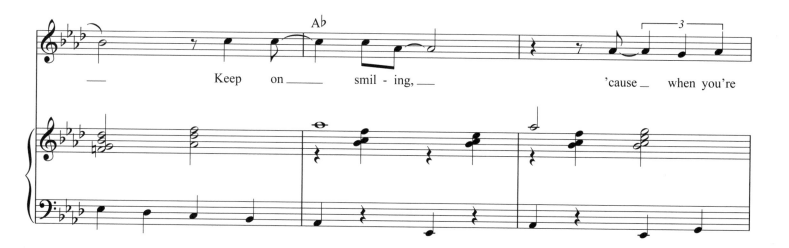

___ Keep on ___ smil - ing, ___ 'cause ___ when you're

smil - ing _____ a - the whole world

smiles _____ with you. ___

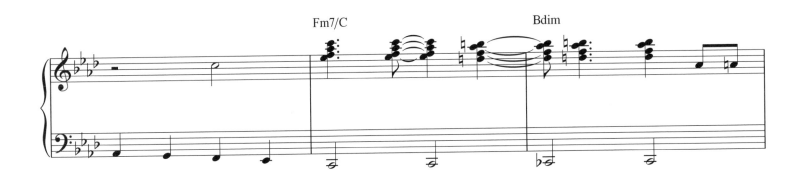

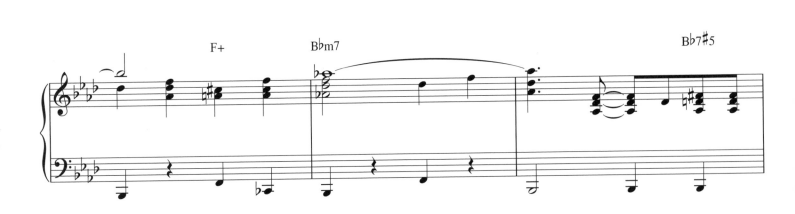

the whole world smiles _____ with you. _

When you're __

___ smil - ing
(when you're   smil - ing),

when you're   smil - ing (keep   on

smil - ing),   a - the   whole   world   smiles   with   you. _

bring on the rain. Stop that

sigh - ing; come on, be hap - py a - gain.

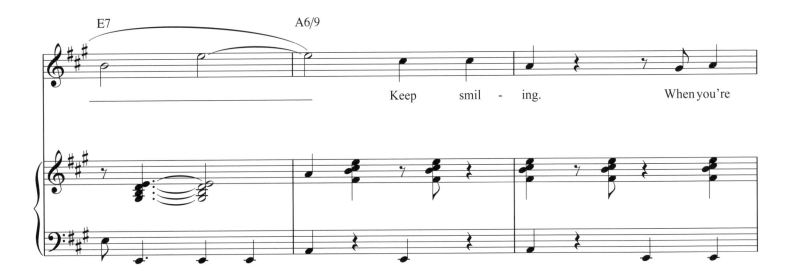

Keep smil - ing. When you're

smil - ing, ba - by, the whole world,

WHERE OR WHEN

Words by LORENZ HART
Music by RICHARD RODGERS

seems that ___ we have met be - fore, and

laughed ___ be - fore, and loved ___ be -

fore, but who knows where or

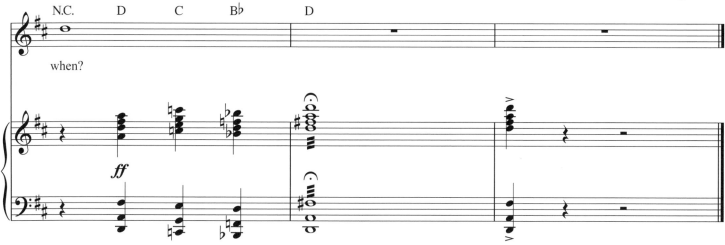

when?

ORIGINAL KEYS FOR SINGERS

Titles in the Original Keys for Singers series are designed for vocalists looking for authentic transcriptions from their favorite artists. The books transcribe famous vocal performances exactly as recorded and provide piano accompaniment parts so that you can perform or pratice exactly as Ella or Patsy or Josh!

ACROSS THE UNIVERSE
00307010..$19.95

ADELE
00155395..$19.99

LOUIS ARMSTRONG
00307029..$19.99

THE BEATLES
00307400..$19.99

BROADWAY HITS (FEMALE SINGERS)
00119085..$19.99

BROADWAY HITS (MALE SINGERS)
00119084..$19.99

PATSY CLINE
00740072..$22.99

ELLA FITZGERALD
00740252..$17.99

JOSH GROBAN
00306969..$19.99

BILLIE HOLIDAY
Transcribed from Historic Recordings
00740140..$19.99

ETTA JAMES: GREATEST HITS
00130427..$19.99

JAZZ DIVAS
00114959..$19.99

LADIES OF CHRISTMAS
00312192..$19.99

NANCY LAMOTT
00306995..$19.99

MEN OF CHRISTMAS
00312241..$19.99

THE BETTE MIDLER SONGBOOK
00307067..$19.99

THE BEST OF LIZA MINNELLI
00306928..$19.99

ONCE
00102569..$16.99

ELVIS PRESLEY
00138200..$19.99

SHOWSTOPPERS FOR FEMALE SINGERS
00119640..$19.99

BEST OF NINA SIMONE
00121576..$19.99

FRANK SINATRA – MORE OF HIS BEST
00307081..$19.99

TAYLOR SWIFT
00142702..$16.99

SARAH VAUGHAN
00306558..$19.99

VOCAL POP
00312656..$19.99

ANDY WILLIAMS – CHRISTMAS COLLECTION
00307158..$17.99

ANDY WILLIAMS
00307160..$17.99

HAL•LEONARD®
www.halleonard.com

Prices, contents, and availability subject to change without notice.